DK Spot the
Bird

Joseph DiCostanzo

LONDON, NEW YORK, MUNICH,
MELBOURNE, AND DELHI

Editor	Lizzie Munsey
US Editor	Jill Hamilton
Senior Art Editor	Jacqui Swan
Project Art Editor	Duncan Turner
Designer	Fiona Macdonald
Production Editor	Ben Marcus
Production Controller	Erika Pepe
Jacket Designer	Mark Cavanagh
Jacket Editor	Manisha Majithia
Managing Art Editor	Michelle Baxter
Managing Editor	Camilla Hallinan
Publisher	Sarah Larter
Art Director	Philip Ormerod
Associate Publishing Director	Liz Wheeler
Publishing Director	Jonathan Metcalf

First published in 2012 by DK Publishing
375 Hudson Street, New York,
New York 10014

12 13 14 15 10 9 8 7 6 5 4 3 2 1
001 – 183838 – May/2012

DK books are available at special discounts when purchased in bulk for sc
promotions, premiums, fund-raising, or educational use. For details, conta
DK Publishing Special Markets, 375 Hudson Street, New York, New York 100
or SpecialSales@dk.com.

Printed and bound in China
by South China Printing Company (Ltd)

Discover more at
www.dk.com

Stickers

Once you have seen a bird, find its sticker at
the back of the book and add it to the page.

Seen it!

Seen it!

Contents

**Plus over 100 stickers
at the back**

Icons

♂ This symbol is used to show when a male bird
is pictured, if the female looks different.

♀ This symbol is used to show when a female
bird is pictured, if the male looks different.

Habitat—where
the bird lives

Food—what
the bird eats

Length—from
tail to bill

Where are they?

Birds are everywhere, but there are more birds in some places than in others. You will usually see more birds near water.

Towns and cities

Some birds are quite happy with urban life. Pigeons are common in towns and cities, and even birds of prey such as Peregrine Falcons have been seen nesting on tall buildings and bridges in cities.

Gardens

If there is a garden where you live, you can start birdwatching by looking out of the window. You can encourage more birds to come to your garden by giving them food, water, or nest boxes (see pages 12–13).

Rivers and lakes

Wherever they live, birds all need to drink and wash. Some birds live on the water. Many eat insects and other things that live in or near water. You will usually see more birds near water.

Woodland

Many birds live in woods, and leafy summer trees are easy places for birds to hide in. This makes it much harder to see them in the woods. You will probably hear more birds than you see.

Seashore

Some birds mostly live near the sea, and nest on cliffs. Others walk along the shore in search of food. Look out for gulls, terns, and sandpipers.

Which bird?

Birds can be hard to tell apart. To help you learn which bird you are looking at, look first at its size, then its shape, then its color.

Size
If you see a bird you don't know, try to compare it to a bird you do know, starting with its size.

House Sparrow
small

Rock Pigeon
medium

Mallard
large

Tundra Swan
huge

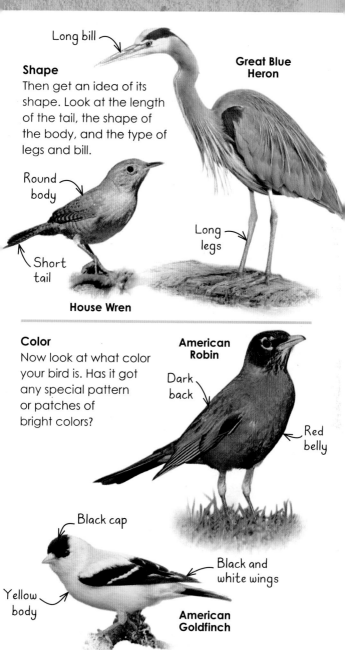

Long bill

Great Blue Heron

Shape
Then get an idea of its shape. Look at the length of the tail, the shape of the body, and the type of legs and bill.

Round body

Short tail

Long legs

House Wren

Color
Now look at what color your bird is. Has it got any special pattern or patches of bright colors?

American Robin

Dark back

Red belly

Black cap

Black and white wings

Yellow body

American Goldfinch

Behavior

The way a bird behaves is often because of what it eats and how it gets its food. Watching bird behavior can help you identify birds.

White-throated Sparrow

This bird eats small seeds and insects from the ground. It frequently whistles its song—*old Sam Peabody, Peabody, Peabody.*

Great Blue Heron

Herons eat fish, which they catch with their bills. You see them standing at the water's edge or walking slowly and quietly, ready to snatch any fish that swims past.

House Sparrows

House Sparrows love to be in noisy little flocks. They squabble and chirrup while they feed next to each other, eating seeds and tiny insects.

Strong bill for drilling holes

Short legs and sharp claws for clinging onto the tree

Downy Woodpecker

Woodpeckers are specially suited to living in trees. The Downy Woodpecker makes holes in trees for its nests, and eats insects that it finds in the bark.

Tail is used as prop against the tree

Watch them fly

All North American birds can fly.
How they fly and the shape of their
wings and tail can help you identify
them when they are in the air (see
also pages 68–69).

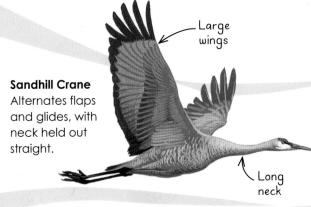

Large
wings

Sandhill Crane
Alternates flaps
and glides, with
neck held out
straight.

Long
neck

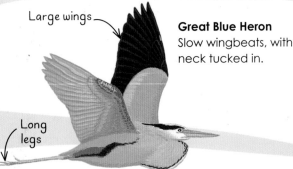

Large wings

Great Blue Heron
Slow wingbeats, with
neck tucked in.

Long
legs

Blurred wings

Ruby-throated Hummingbird
Hovers in front of flowers, and
can fly backward.

Tiny
body

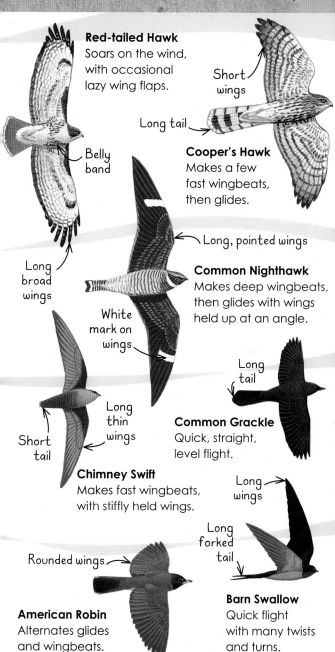

Red-tailed Hawk
Soars on the wind, with occasional lazy wing flaps.

Short wings

Long tail

Belly band

Cooper's Hawk
Makes a few fast wingbeats, then glides.

Long, pointed wings

Long broad wings

White mark on wings

Common Nighthawk
Makes deep wingbeats, then glides with wings held up at an angle.

Long tail

Common Grackle
Quick, straight, level flight.

Long thin wings

Short tail

Chimney Swift
Makes fast wingbeats, with stiffly held wings.

Long wings

Long forked tail

Rounded wings

Barn Swallow
Quick flight with many twists and turns.

American Robin
Alternates glides and wingbeats.

In the garden

Gardens are great places to see birds. You can encourage more birds to visit your garden by giving them food, water, and somewhere to shelter.

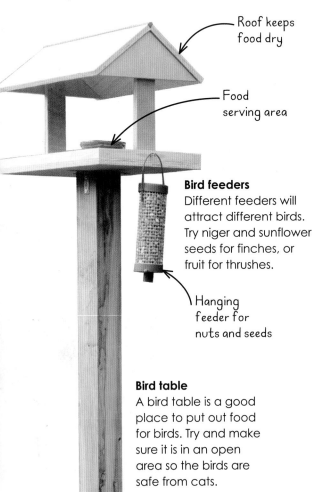

Roof keeps food dry

Food serving area

Bird feeders
Different feeders will attract different birds. Try niger and sunflower seeds for finches, or fruit for thrushes.

Hanging feeder for nuts and seeds

Bird table
A bird table is a good place to put out food for birds. Try and make sure it is in an open area so the birds are safe from cats.

Rose hips

Plants

Some plants will attract
more birds than others.
Sunflowers are good, but
bushes with seeds and
berries are best. Lawns
are good places for
birds to find worms.

Small hole for
bluebirds and
sparrows

Bird box

These boxes give birds
somewhere to build
their nests. They come
in many shapes
and sizes, which are
good for different birds.

Bird bath

A small bird
bath gives birds
clean water to
drink as well as
somewhere to
wash. They need
to wash to keep
their feathers
clean and
healthy.

Useful words

Bar
A plumage mark that crosses a bird's body, wing, or tail.

Bill or beak
The nose and mouth of a bird. It has no teeth and a tough, stiff covering like a fingernail.

Bird of prey
A bird with a hooked bill, which kills and eats other animals.

Birding
Finding and watching wild birds as a hobby.

Call
Each type of bird makes sounds that are different from other birds. Calls are simple notes that help them keep in touch.

Chick
A baby bird, before it can fly.

Conifer
A tree with sharp, needlelike leaves and seeds hidden in cones. Some birds live only in coniferous forests.

Crest
A tuft of feathers on a bird's head that it can lift up like a fan or spike.

Flock
A group of birds.

Glide
The part of flight where a bird keeps its outstretched wings still in between wingbeats.

Immature
A bird that is old enough to fly, but is not yet an adult.

Juvenile
A young bird in its very first plumage.

Migration
A long journey made twice a year, between summer and winter areas.

Molt
The changing of old feathers for new ones. Most birds molt their feathers twice a year.

Plumage
The feathers on a bird. Also the pattern on a bird's feathers, which may be different in summer and winter or different for male and female birds.

Predator
An animal that eats other animals.

Prey
An animal that is eaten by other animals.

Roost
To sleep (for a bird). Also a place where birds sleep.

Song
Each bird has its own song, which tells you which bird it is. The song is longer than a call and helps birds defend their nests. It also helps male birds attract females as mates.

Streak
A plumage mark that runs lengthwise along a bird's body.

Trill
One note that is repeated quickly many times in a row as part of a bird's song or call.

Warble
A bird's song that flows along musically, like a whistle or flute.

Wingbeat
A flap of a bird's wings.

Wingtip
The point or end of the wing: the two wingtips lie alongside the tail when the wings are closed.

Parts of birds

All birds have feathers. These grow in rows and patches and give a bird its color and patterns. The feathers are molted once or twice a year. Some birds' plumage changes as they get older, and some birds change from summer to winter colors.

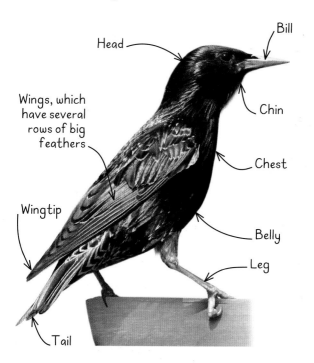

Head

Bill

Chin

Wings, which have several rows of big feathers

Chest

Wingtip

Belly

Leg

Tail

Black cap

White cheek

Gray back

Black chin

Noisy and busy
Listen for chickadees calling their name—*tscik-a-dee-dee-dee*. They are active little birds, always moving.

Friendly bird
Titmice are often found with their smaller cousins, the chickadees. Listen for their loud song—*peter, peter, peter*.

Crest

Gray back

Pale gray belly

Orange-brown sides

Black-capped Chickadee

Chickadees are often found at bird feeders. In winter they form flocks with one another and with other small birds.

Woods, gardens

Insects, seeds

5¼ in (13.5 cm)

Seen it!

Tufted Titmouse

Titmice are very tame and curious and sometimes come to look if you make squeaky noises. They visit gardens for food.

Woods, gardens

Insects, seeds

6½ in (17 cm)

Seen it!

Gray
cap

Black
chin

Gray
chest
and
belly

♂

Noisy friends
You often hear House Sparrows
before you see them. They like
to be together in noisy groups.
Females are plainer than males.

White line
on wing

Gray
eyebrow

Brown
streaks on
gray back

Rounded
tail

Brown
streaks on
white belly

Chest spot
Besides their many
streaks, Song Sparrows
often have a dark,
spot on the center
of their chests.

House Sparrow

These birds were brought to America by European colonists, to remind them of home. They are now found all over North America.

Towns, villages

Seeds, fruit, insects

5½ in (14 cm)

Seen it!

Song Sparrow

This is probably the most common sparrow in North America. There are many local types, which are slightly different sizes and shades of brown.

Marshes, fields, towns

Insects, seeds

6½ i (17 c

Seen it!

Chipping Sparrow

These small sparrows are often found in flocks on lawns and grassy fields. Young birds have streaked caps.

Bright brown cap

Gray face

Black line through eye

Seen it!

Lark Sparrow

This is one of the largest American sparrows. It is found west of the Mississippi River. Look out for its bold head pattern.

Brown and white stripe on head

Black stripes on head

Seen it!

Black spot chest

White on outside of tail

White-throated Sparrow
This sparrow breeds in woods in the north. Its small white chin patch is often harder to see than its light and dark head stripes.

Yellow spot behind bill

Long tail

White chin

Seen it!

House Wren
This small, plain-looking bird has a lovely, bubbly song of many whistled notes. It uses nest boxes for shelter in the winter.

Pale eyebrow

Dark lines on wings and tail

Seen it!

Long tail

Dark cap

Gray body

Gray face

Brown under tail

Summer singer
In the summer, listen for the musical song of the catbird. It is named for its kittenlike *mew* call.

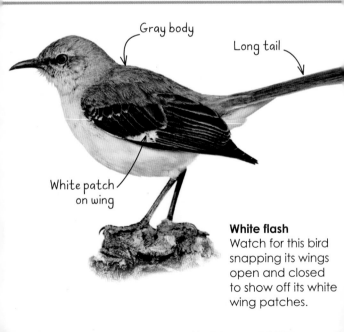

Gray body

Long tail

White patch on wing

White flash
Watch for this bird snapping its wings open and closed to show off its white wing patches.

Gray Catbird

These shy birds can be hard to spot, as they like to live in dense bushes. They are only found east of the Rocky Mountains.

Woods, gardens

Berries, insects

Seen it!

9 in
(23 cm)

Northern Mockingbird

Mockingbirds make up songs by copying other birds and any other noises they hear. They often sing at night.

Hedges, gardens

Berries, insects

Seen it!

10 in
(25½ cm)

Yellow bill

White around eye

Head turner
Robins turn their heads to the side when they look for food on the ground. People used to think they were listening for worms.

Dark back

Reddish chest and belly

American Robin

These are among the first birds to sing in the morning. Young robins have pale bellies with dark spots.

Woods, gardens

Worms, fruit, insects

10 in (25½ cm)

Seen it!

Tail pumper

Hermit Thrushes like to pump their tails slowly up and down. They are usually the first thrushes to arrive in the spring.

White around eye

Dark brown back

Dark spots on chest

Bright brown tail

Hermit Thrush

This bird has a beautiful, flutelike song that can be heard from a long way away. Listen for it in the woods.

Woods

Insects, worms

6½ in (17 cm)

Seen it!

Long black bill

Loud call
The loud caw, caw of the American Crow is one of the most familiar bird calls. It can be heard from a great distance.

All black body

Strong legs and feet

American Crow

In some places, crows meet in winter flocks of thousands. They are very aggressive and sometimes attack other birds.

Woods, towns

Fruit, eggs, insects

18 in (47 cm)

Seen it!

Changing colors
In the winter, Starlings are covered with white spots and their pointed bills are black. Young birds are plain gray-brown in the late summer.

Pointed yellow bill

Shiny purple-black body

Pink legs and feet

Short square tail

European Starling

Starlings were brought to New York City from Europe in the 1890s. They are now found across the US.

Towns, farms

Insects, seeds, berries

8½ in (21 cm)

Seen it!

Black mask

Greenish back

Yellow throat

Pale belly

♂

Masked singer
Male yellowthroats sing *witchity witchity witchity which*. Females have no masks and do not sing. In the fall, young males have only partial masks.

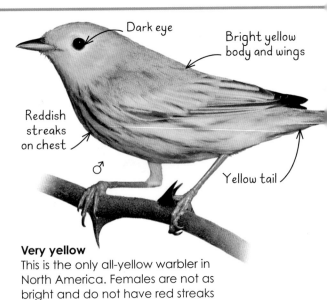

Dark eye

Bright yellow body and wings

Reddish streaks on chest

♂

Yellow tail

Very yellow
This is the only all-yellow warbler in North America. Females are not as bright and do not have red streaks on the chest and belly.

Common Yellowthroat

Yellowthroats usually stay low to the ground, but in the spring males sometimes sing from high perches.

Marshes, woods

Insects, seeds

5 in (13 cm)

Seen it!

Yellow Warbler

Look for this common warbler in the summer. It can be found in open woods almost anywhere in North America. Its song is made up of fast, changing notes.

Woods, gardens

Insects

5 in (13 cm)

Seen it!

American Redstart
Female redstarts look similar to the males, but are gray and yellow instead of black and orange.

Orange patch on wing

Dark head and back

Orange sides ♂

Orange on tail

Seen it!

Magnolia Warbler
These birds nest in conifer forests in the north and are common visitors to the eastern US. Females and young are plainer than males.

Gray cap

White patch on wing

Black streaks on yellow chest ♂

Seen it!

Yellow-rumped Warbler

This is one of the few warblers that spends the winter in the US. Yellow-rumps have white throats in the east, and yellow throats in the west.

Yellow above tail

Seen it!

Dark streaks on chest

Yellow sides

♂

Black-and-white Warbler

These warblers creep along tree trunks and large branches, looking for insects in the bark. Females have white throats.

Black and white stripes on head

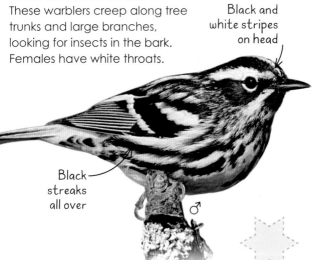

Black streaks all over

♂

Seen it!

Bright red
head and body

Red male
Adult male Summer
Tanagers are bright red.
One-year-old males are
blotchy, and females are
mostly yellow-green.

Red
wings

♂

Red tail

Summer Tanager

Summer Tanagers leave the United
States for winter, and go to the
warm forests of South America.

Woods

Insects,
fruit

8 in
(20 cm)

Seen it!

Eastern beauty
Look for this striking tanager in the summer —you will see it in the tops of trees in the east. Females are dull yellow-green, and males look like the females in the fall.

Bright red head and body

Black tail

Black wings

♂

Scarlet Tanager

The male Scarlet Tanager has a loud *CHIP-burr* call, that can be heard in the forest from a long way away.

Woods

Insects, fruit

7 in (18 cm)

Seen it!

Black-headed Grosbeak

Look for this large-billed bird in woods west of the Great Plains in the summer. Females are much plainer than males.

Black head

Large thick bill

White patches on wing

Orange belly

♂

Seen it!

Rose-breasted Grosbeak

This is the eastern cousin of the Black-headed Grosbeak. Females have brown backs and head stripes. Both of these grosbeaks go to Central America for the winter.

Black head and back

Large thick b

Pink chest

White belly

♂

Seen it!

White patches on wing

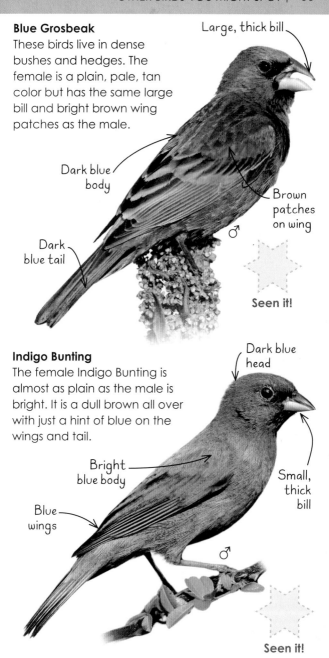

Blue Grosbeak

These birds live in dense bushes and hedges. The female is a plain, pale, tan color but has the same large bill and bright brown wing patches as the male.

Large, thick bill

Dark blue body

Brown patches on wing

Dark blue tail

♂

Seen it!

Indigo Bunting

The female Indigo Bunting is almost as plain as the male is bright. It is a dull brown all over with just a hint of blue on the wings and tail.

Dark blue head

Bright blue body

Small, thick bill

Blue wings

♂

Seen it!

Bird groups

Some birds live on their own, but others stay together. Some live in families in the summer and then gather in big flocks in the winter.

Winter gathering
Flocks of Black-capped Chickadees wander through the treetops in fall and winter. They are often joined by other small birds.

Long journey
Some birds meet in huge flocks and migrate long distances for the winter (see pages 102–103). Flocks of Snow Geese fly thousands of miles every year.

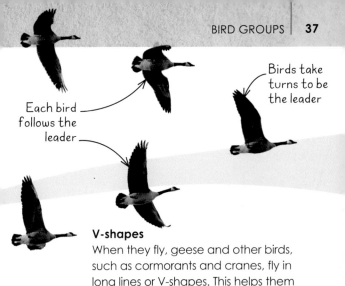

Birds take turns to be the leader

Each bird follows the leader

V-shapes

When they fly, geese and other birds, such as cormorants and cranes, fly in long lines or V-shapes. This helps them keep in touch with one another. It is also easier to fly through the air just behind and to one side of another bird.

Huge flock

Starlings feed in small flocks but on winter evenings they get together in flocks of tens or hundreds of thousands. The whole flock then sleeps together in a wood or reed bed.

Hidden red

When the Red-wing folds its wings, the red patches can be almost totally hidden. Females and young are brown and have no red patches.

Pointed bill

Red patch with yellow edge on wing

Black body

♂

Red-winged Blackbird

Look for Red-winged Blackbirds near water. They form large flocks when they are ready to migrate.

Marshes, swamps

Seeds, insects

8 in (20 cm)

Seen it!

Summer guest
This bird is found in western Canada and the United States in the summer. Females and young have yellow throats not yellow heads.

Black in front of eye

Black body

Long tail

Yellow head and chest

White patch on wing

♂

Yellow-headed Blackbird

Most of these birds go to Mexico for the winter. A few visit the east—you would be very lucky to spot one!

Marshes, fields

Seeds, insects

9 in (22 cm)

Seen it!

Shiny head

The male Grackle's head ca shine in the sun. Some birds have shiny purple backs, and others are shiny green. Females are less shiny.

Shiny purplish head

Long pointed bill

Brownish back

Long tail

♂

Common Grackle

In the winter, grackles and other blackbirds gather in huge flocks, which sometimes have a million birds.

Woods, parks

Insects, seeds

12 in (30 cm)

Seen it!

Musical repeater
Brown Thrashers sing
complicated songs. They
repeat each set of notes in
their songs twice.

Gray cheek

Bright
brown back

Dark streaks
on white
chest and
belly

Long tail

Brown Thrasher

This bird is shy and easy to miss. It likes
to stay in dense tangles and hedges,
except when it perches up high to sing.

Woods,
hedges

Insects,
berries

11 in
(27 cm)

Seen it!

Orange-gold and yellow on top of head

Light line above eye

Greenish back

White line on wing ♂

Hidden Gold
The male kinglet usually hides the orange on his head under the yellow. He raises the yellow feathers to show the orange to the female.

White ring around eye

Blue-gray back

Long black tail with white edge

White throat

Pale belly ♂

Treetop birds
These tiny birds spend nearly all their time in the tops of the trees. Males have a black line over the eye, and males and females often hold their tails up.

Golden-crowned Kinglet

Kinglets like to flick their wings open and closed. They move around the trees looking for insects.

Woods, parks

Insects

4 in (10 cm)

Seen it!

Blue-gray Gnatcatcher

The best way to find gnatcatchers is to listen for their frequent, thin sounding, high-pitched call—*zhee, zhee*.

Woods

Insects

4½ in (11 cm)

Seen it!

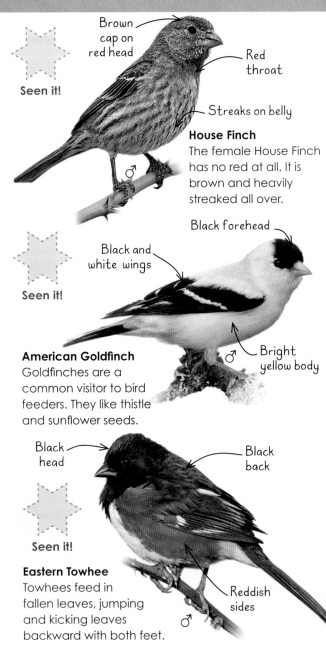

Brown cap on red head

Red throat

Streaks on belly

Seen it!

House Finch
The female House Finch has no red at all. It is brown and heavily streaked all over.

Black forehead

Black and white wings

Seen it!

American Goldfinch
Goldfinches are a common visitor to bird feeders. They like thistle and sunflower seeds.

♂ Bright yellow body

Black head

Black back

Seen it!

Eastern Towhee
Towhees feed in fallen leaves, jumping and kicking leaves backward with both feet.

♂ Reddish sides

Gray body

Pink bill

Seen it!

Dark-eyed Junco
These winter visitors have a few different color patterns in the west. Some have black heads, some pink sides, and some bright brown backs.

Black head and back

Seen it!

Orange belly

♂

Baltimore Oriole
Orioles build hanging nests at the end of branches. They are easily seen in the fall when trees are bare.

Eastern Phoebe
This plain bird wags its tail and says its name, *fee-bee*, in the spring.

Dark cap

Dark back

Pale belly

Seen it!

Out in the open
Bluebirds like to perch in the open, on tree branches, fences, and telephone lines. Females are not as bright as males and young birds have spots.

Bright blue back

Reddish throat and chest

White belly

♂

Noisy and common
The loud *jay, jay, jay* call of the Blue Jay is a familiar sound in forests, towns, and cities in the east.

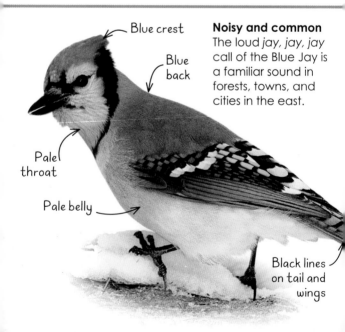

Blue crest

Blue back

Pale throat

Pale belly

Black lines on tail and wings

Eastern Bluebird

This bluebird can be found on the edges of woods and around orchards east of the Rocky Mountains.

Woods

Insects, fruit

7 in
(18 cm)

Seen it!

Blue Jay

Jays sometimes form mobs of birds around birds of prey such as hawks and owls. They call loudly at the bigger birds, trying to chase them away.

Woods, gardens

Insects, nuts, fruit

11 in
(27 cm)

Seen it!

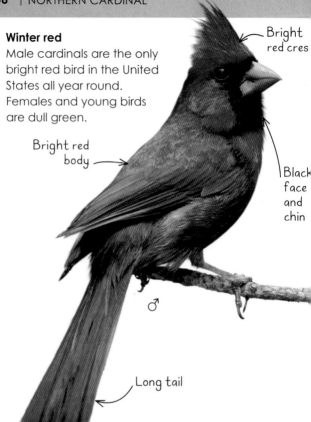

Winter red
Male cardinals are the only
bright red bird in the United
States all year round.
Females and young birds
are dull green.

Bright red
body →

Bright
red cres[t]

Black
face
and
chin

♂

Long tail

Northern Cardinal

Males cardinals are very aggressive
and will even attack their own
reflections in windows.

Woods,
gardens

Seeds,
insects

8½ in
(22 cm)

Seen it!

Handsome adult
The smooth, silky looks of the adult waxwing make it one of the most attractive and easily recognized birds in North America. Young birds are streaked.

Crest

Black mask

Gray back

Yellow belly

Red on wing

Yellow on end of tail

Cedar Waxwing

Waxwings are almost never alone. If you see one, look around it to find the rest of the flock.

Woods, parks

Berries, insects

7½ in (19 cm)

Seen it!

Western Kingbird

This kingbird is common in summer in the west, but sometimes visits the east in the fall, on its way to Central America.

Gray head

Seen it!

White edge on tail

Yellow belly

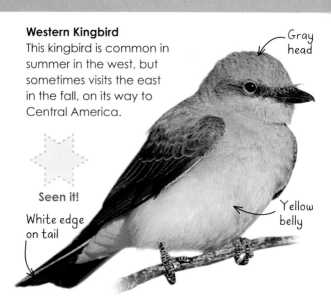

Eastern Kingbird

This kingbird flies out from its perch to catch passing flying insects. It likes to perch high up and in the open.

Black head

Gray back

White throat

White tail tip

Seen it!

Warbling Vireo

This plain little bird is often hard to spot high in the leaves of trees. It doesn't move around much, even when singing its complicated, fast song.

Pale line above eye

Gray back

Seen it!

Pale belly

Red-eyed Vireo

Look out for this vireo's head stripes. You can also listen for its simple three note song.

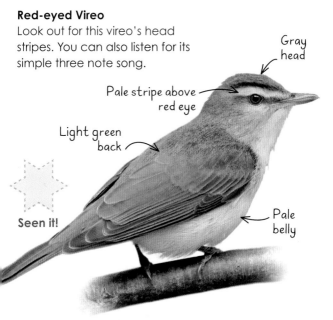

Gray head

Pale stripe above red eye

Light green back

Seen it!

Pale belly

Small head

Small bill

Many patterns
Pigeons come in many different colors and patterns, but are easily recognized by their size and shape.

Very plump body

Dark end of tail

Pink feet

Small head

Slender body

Smaller cousin
This bird is smaller than the Rock Pigeon, with a longer tail and a more slender body. Its *oowoo hoo-hoo-hoo* call is easily mistaken for an owl.

Dark spots on wing

Long tail

Rock Pigeon

These birds were brought to North America by the European colonists. Some people raise them for racing. They eat nearly anything and meet in large flocks.

Towns, cities, farms

Seeds, berries

12 in (30 cm)

Seen it!

Mourning Dove

This well-known bird is found across America, except in deep forest. In cities, it sometimes nests on window ledges and fire escapes.

Towns, farms

Seeds

11 in (27 cm)

Seen it!

Breeding

Different types of birds have different ways of picking a mate, nesting, and then raising their chicks. However, there are some things that most birds do in the same way.

Singing
The male bird often sings in spring and summer to try to attract a female. Singing also tells other males to keep away. Common Yellowthroats have loud songs despite their small size.

Pairing
Many birds choose who they will nest with in complicated ways. Pairs of Western Grebes do dances together on the water.

Nesting

Most birds make nests. The nest is a safe place for the female to lay her eggs and to raise the young. Nests are often made of grass and twigs, but Great Blue Herons make theirs from sticks.

Sitting

Sometimes it is the female that sits on the eggs until they hatch. For other birds, like this Common Loon, both parents take turns sitting on the eggs.

Feeding chicks

The parents bring food to the growing chicks in the nest. Young Pileated Woodpeckers will leave the nest after about four weeks.

Night hunter
Nighthawks catch flying insects at night. Watch for them flying like giant, long-winged moths. Males have white throats.

♀

Gray back

Long pointed wings

Dark lines on belly

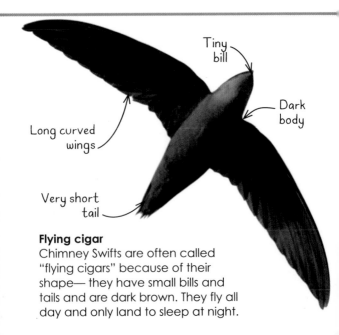

Tiny bill

Dark body

Long curved wings

Very short tail

Flying cigar
Chimney Swifts are often called "flying cigars" because of their shape— they have small bills and tails and are dark brown. They fly all day and only land to sleep at night.

Common Nighthawk

Nighthawks often roost in trees during the day. Their coloring makes them look like a part of the branch.

Fields, towns

Flying insects

9 in (23 cm)

Seen it!

Chimney Swift

These birds are a common sight in the east during the warmer months. Listen for their twittering calls overhead. They spend the winter in South America.

Cities, towns

Flying insects

5 in (13 cm)

Seen it!

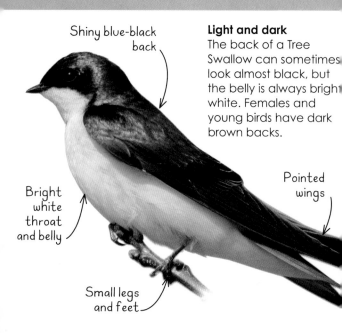

Shiny blue-black back

Light and dark
The back of a Tree Swallow can sometimes look almost black, but the belly is always bright white. Females and young birds have dark brown backs.

Pointed wings

Bright white throat and belly

Small legs and feet

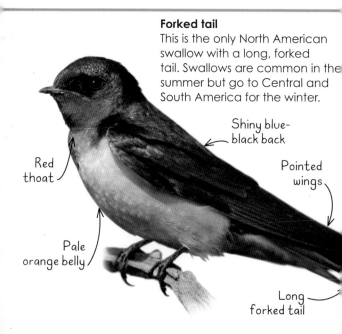

Forked tail
This is the only North American swallow with a long, forked tail. Swallows are common in the summer but go to Central and South America for the winter.

Shiny blue-black back

Red throat

Pointed wings

Pale orange belly

Long forked tail

Tree Swallow

In the fall, these birds gather in large flocks late in the day and roost in marshes. Most Tree Swallows spend the winter in Central America and return in the spring.

Watersides

Flying insects

5 in (13 cm)

Seen it!

Barn Swallow

Barn Swallows got their name from their habit of nesting in barns, sheds, and other buildings. They hunt in the air, catching insects in their wide mouths.

Towns, farms

Flying insects

7 in (17 cm)

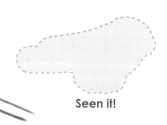

Seen it!

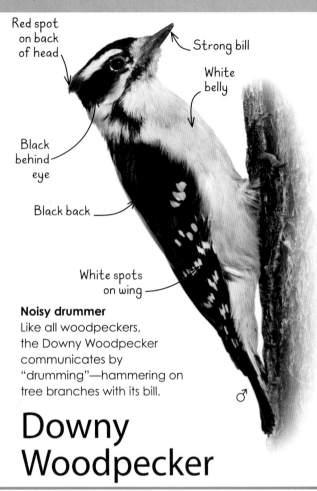

Red spot on back of head

Strong bill

White belly

Black behind eye

Black back

White spots on wing

Noisy drummer
Like all woodpeckers, the Downy Woodpecker communicates by "drumming"—hammering on tree branches with its bill.

♂

Downy Woodpecker

Downy Woodpeckers are North America's smallest and probably most common woodpecker.

Woods, gardens

Insects, spiders

6 in (15 cm)

Seen it!

Red Forehead

Strong bill

White patch on wing

Red throat

Black and white back

Hidden colors
The yellow belly that gives this bird its name is hard to see. Females have white throats and young birds have no red on their heads.

♂

Yellow-bellied Sapsucker

Sapsuckers drill neat rows of holes in tree trunks. They feed on the sap and insects that collect in the holes.

Woods

Sap, insects

8 in (20 cm)

Seen it!

Red head

Black back

White belly

Large white patch on wing

Seen it!

Red-headed Woodpecker

This is the only woodpecker in America with an all-red head. It is found east of the Rocky Mountains. Young birds have brown heads and backs.

Red crest

Black belly

Black stripe on face

Black back and wings

Seen it!

Pileated Woodpecker

The largest woodpecker in North America, the Pileated is the size of a crow. It lives in large forests with lots of dead trees.

♂

Black chest

Seen it!

Dark bars on
brown back

Dark spots
on belly

Northern Flicker
In the east, flickers
have yellow under
their wings and
males have a black
mustache. In the west
they have red under
the wing and males
have a red mustache.

♂

Horned Lark
These larks have lovely,
musical songs. They sing
from the ground or
while flying. Look for
them on the ground in
prairies and deserts.

Tiny feather
horns

Yellow
face

Seen it!

Thin curved bill

Light streaks on brown back

Pale belly

Moving bark
These small birds look like a piece of tree bark that has decided to creep up the trunk of a tree. They move up one tree, then fly to the bottom of another tree and start again.

Long tail

Brown Creeper

Creepers use their long, stiff tails to prop themselves up on tree trunks as they search for insects.

Woods

Insects

5¼ in
(14.5 cm)

Seen it!

Tree lover
Nuthatches look for insects along the trunks and main branches of trees. They move up, down, sideways, and even hang upside down.

Long pointy bill

Black cap

White face

Dark gray back

White belly

♂

Short tail

White-breasted Nuthatch

Nuthatches often visit birdfeeders during the winter months. Females have gray caps.

Woods

Insects

5¾ in (14.5 cm)

Seen it!

Tiny jewels
These shiny, tiny gems are the smallest birds in eastern North America. The male's red throat can look black at some angles. Females have white chins and throats.

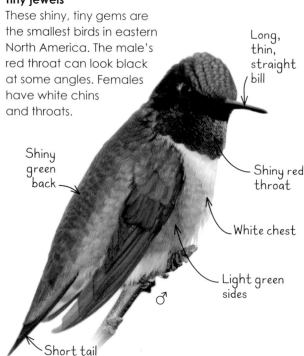

Long, thin, straight bill

Shiny green back

Shiny red throat

White chest

Light green sides

♂

Short tail

Ruby-throated Hummingbird

In spring, the male Ruby-throated Hummingbird displays to the female by flying up and down in giant U-shapes in front of her.

Woods, gardens

Nectar, insects

3½ in (9 cm)

Seen it!

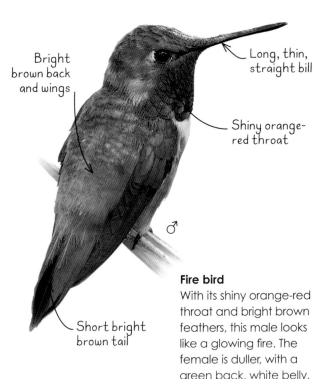

Bright brown back and wings

Long, thin, straight bill

Shiny orange-red throat

♂

Short bright brown tail

Fire bird

With its shiny orange-red throat and bright brown feathers, this male looks like a glowing fire. The female is duller, with a green back, white belly, and streaked throat.

Rufous Hummingbird

This hummingbird is common in the west in the summer. It nests as far north as Alaska.

Woods, gardens

Nectar, insects

3½ in (9 cm)

Seen it!

Flight styles

Birds do not all fly in the same way. Every bird has a flight pattern, which is different depending on how often it flaps its wings or holds them still to glide along.

Pileated Woodpecker
Woodpeckers make fast bursts of wingbeats, then rise up before closing their wings to make deep downward swoops.

Barn Swallow
Swallows make many turns and swoops, with bursts of smooth wingbeats between glides.

Great Blue Heron
Herons and egrets fly in straight lines with slow and steady wingbeats.

Mallard
Ducks beat their wings fast and steadily, and only glide when they come down to land on land or water.

Speedy bird
This southwestern bird can run fast, and can also fly when it wants to. No other bird in North America looks like it.

Large bill

Crest

Very long tail

Streaks on chest

Strong legs and feet

Tail fanned out to attract females

No feathe on head

Red, wrinkl skin o neck

Shiny feathers on body

♂

Greater Roadrunner

Unlike the cartoon, the real roadrunner does not call "beep, beep," but makes cooing sounds, like a dove.

Deserts, open country

Lizards, insects

21 in (53 cm)

Seen it!

Wild Turkey

These birds were given their name by mistake. When they were first brought to Europe from America, people thought they had come from Turkey.

Woods, fields

Acorns, nuts

3 ft (1 m)

Native American
The Wild Turkey is only found in America. The male's *gobble gobble* call is well known.

Seen it!

Night hooter
This owl calls at night. It makes three or more deep hoots, which are easy to identify and can be heard from a long way away.

Large ear tufts

Yellow eyes

White chin

Large chunky body

Dark bars on belly

Great Horned Owl

These owls nest earlier than any other bird. They sometimes lay their eggs in January.

Woods, towns, parks, deserts

Small animals, insects

21 in (50 cm)

Seen it!

Question call
When Barred Owls call, they sound like they are asking you a question—*who-cooks-for-you, who-cooks-for-you-all?*

Round head

Dark eyes

Yelllow bill

Dark streaks on belly

Dark bars on chest

Barred Owl

This owl is usually active at night, but it sometimes hunts and calls during the day.

Woods, swamps

Small animals, insects

18 in (46 cm)

Seen it!

Belly band
Red-tailed Hawks have
a band of dark streaks
across the middle of their
bellies. Only adults have
bright reddish tails, but
all ages have the
belly band.

White
spots on
back

Reddish
tail

Red-tailed Hawk

These hawks are found everywhere,
even in large cities. Watch for them
circling around in the air.

Deserts,
fields, woods

Small animals,
birds

22 in
(58 cm)

Seen it!

Reddish belly
Adult Cooper's Hawks have reddish brown bars on their chests and bellies. Young birds have white chests and bellies with brown streaks.

Dark cap

Gray back

Dark bands on gray tail

Long tail with rounded corners

Cooper's Hawk

These hawks fly by making a few rapid flaps of their wings, then holding them open and still to glide.

Woods

Small animals, birds

16 in (42 cm)

Seen it!

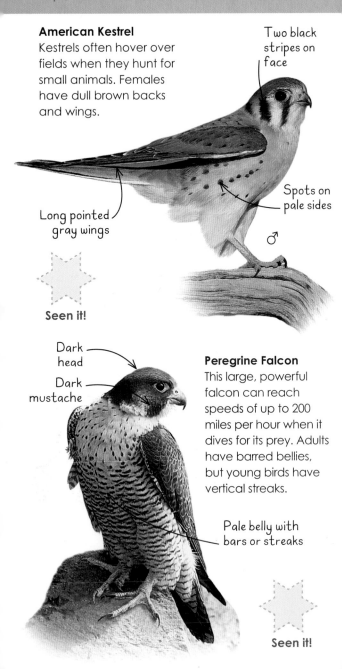

American Kestrel
Kestrels often hover over fields when they hunt for small animals. Females have dull brown backs and wings.

Two black stripes on face

Long pointed gray wings

Spots on pale sides

♂

Seen it!

Dark head

Dark mustache

Peregrine Falcon
This large, powerful falcon can reach speeds of up to 200 miles per hour when it dives for its prey. Adults have barred bellies, but young birds have vertical streaks.

Pale belly with bars or streaks

Seen it!

Northern Harrier

This bird has a white patch above its tail, which you can see when it flies. Adult males have pale gray backs, and females and young have dark brown backs.

Long wings

Pale spotted belly

Long yellow legs

♂

Seen it!

Turkey Vulture

Turkey Vultures are usually seen circling overhead, looking for their next meal. They are often in small groups.

No feathers on head

Dark brown body

Long pink legs

Seen it!

Not bald
These eagles are not really bald. The name comes from the all-white head of the adults. Young birds have dark brown heads and tails.

Large, yellow, hooked bill

Dark brown wings and body

White tail

Yellow legs and feet

Bald Eagle

Bald Eagles mainly eat dead animals and fish, but they also steal fish from Ospreys.

Woods near water

Dead animals, fish

32 in (82 cm)

Seen it!

Fish hawk

Look for Ospreys anywhere where there is water with lots of fish. Seen from below, their long wings are pale with a dark line along them.

Dark stripe behind eye

Yellow eye

Dark brown back

Brown streaks on chest

White belly

Osprey

Ospreys grab fish from the water as they fly along, or dive feet first into the water.

Near water

Fish

22 in (55 cm)

Seen it!

Feeding

Food provides energy for all birds. Some of the biggest birds can go for days without food. Some small birds must eat almost as much as they weigh every day.

Long pointy bill

American Woodcock

Bills

Birds' bills give you clues about what they eat. Grosbeaks use their thick bills to split seeds. Woodcocks use theirs to push into mud and pull out worms. Hawks and falcons tear their prey apart.

Short hooked bill

Peregrine Falcon

Triangular bill

Blue Grosbeak

Strong stomach

Grebes swallow some of their own feathers. These line their stomachs and stop sharp fish bones from poking through.

Feet

Birds' legs and feet show how they get to their food. Shorebirds wade in water. Woodpeckers hang onto branches and tree trunks. Hawks use their claws to catch the animals they eat.

Strong feet

Yellow-bellied Sapsucker

Curved claws

Greater Yellowlegs

Long legs

Osprey

Long toes

Dabbling ducks

Some ducks put their heads under water, then suck in a mouthful of water. They then push the water out with their tongues, keeping any food from the water behind in their mouths.

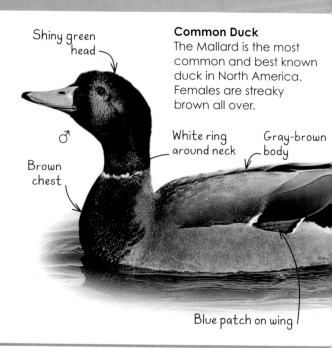

Shiny green head

♂

Brown chest

White ring around neck

Gray-brown body

Blue patch on wing

Common Duck
The Mallard is the most common and best known duck in North America. Females are streaky brown all over.

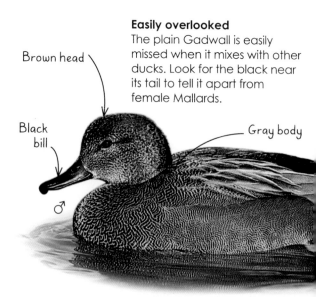

Brown head

Black bill

♂

Gray body

Easily overlooked
The plain Gadwall is easily missed when it mixes with other ducks. Look for the black near its tail to tell it apart from female Mallards.

Mallard

Look for these ducks wherever there is freshwater— even on small ponds and streams. Mallards form large flocks, often with other ducks.

Ponds, watersides

Insects, plants

22 in (55 cm)

Seen it!

Gadwall

Female Gadwalls look a lot like female Mallards. Gadwalls have white spots on their wings, which you can see when they fly or move their wings.

Ponds, marshes

Plants, insects

20 in (50 cm)

Black tail

Seen it!

Northern Shoveler

Groups of these ducks often feed together. They swim in a circle, with their heads held low and flat and their bills in the water.

Seen it!

Large bill shaped like a shovel

Green head

♂

Black tail

Bright brown sides

White chest

Northern Pintail

This duck has a very long tail. The female is a mottled brown color with a shorter tail than the male, but its tail and neck are still longer than other ducks.

Seen it!

Brown head

Long pointy tail

♂

White chest

Green-winged Teal
This small duck has a green wing patch that can be hard to see on the brown females.

Seen it!

Green patch on brown head

Green patch on wing

White stripe on side

Gray body ♂

Lesser Scaup
In the summer, these ducks nest in Alaska and across most of Canada. In the winter, look for them in the southern United States and along the coasts.

Seen it!

Dark head

Gray back

♂

Black chest

Bufflehead

This is the smallest diving duck in
North America. Females are
mostly gray-brown with a small
white cheek patch.

Seen it!

White patch
on black head

Black back

♂

White chest
and belly

Ruddy Duck

This small diving duck has a large
head for its size. It often holds its
long, stiff tail upward
at an angle.

Seen it!

Bright
brown body

White cheek
on dark head

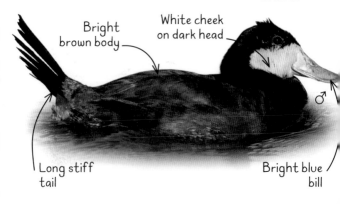

♂

Long stiff
tail

Bright blue
bill

Wood Duck

The male Wood Duck has a striking head pattern. The female is much plainer, with a large white patch around the eye.

Seen it!

Shiny dark green head

Red eye

Long drooping crest

♂

White chin

American Wigeon

Male wigeons have a wheezy call that sounds like a plastic squeeze toy. Females look like males, but plainer.

Seen it!

Green patch on pale head

♂

Black tail

Brown chest and sides

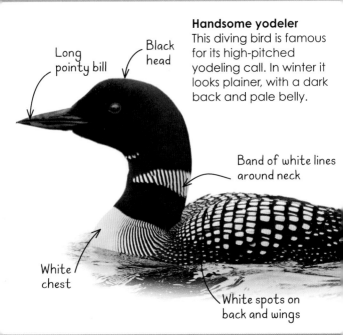

Long pointy bill

Black head

Handsome yodeler
This diving bird is famous for its high-pitched yodeling call. In winter it looks plainer, with a dark back and pale belly.

Band of white lines around neck

White chest

White spots on back and wings

Long, thin, pointy bill

Black head

Black and white
This bird is black and white except for its red eyes and greenish yellow bill. In the summer, it is found on freshwater marshes and lakes. It spends the winter on the Pacific Ocean.

Red eye

Long neck

Dark back

White throat and chest

Common Loon

Loons legs are so far back on their bodies that they cannot walk on land. Instead, they push themselves along on their chests.

Lakes, oceans

Fish, crabs

34 in (75 cm)

Seen it!

Western Grebe

Male and female Western Grebes pair up in the spring. The pair do spectacular and complicated dances together before they mate.

Lakes, ocean, marshes

Fish, crabs

26 in (65 cm)

Seen it!

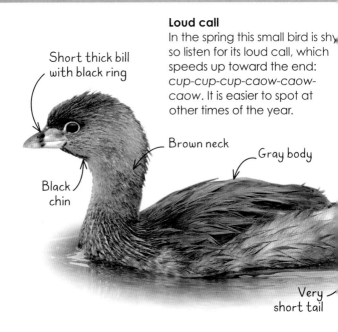

Loud call

In the spring this small bird is shy, so listen for its loud call, which speeds up toward the end: *cup-cup-cup-caow-caow-caow*. It is easier to spot at other times of the year.

Short thick bill with black ring

Brown neck

Gray body

Black chin

Very short tail

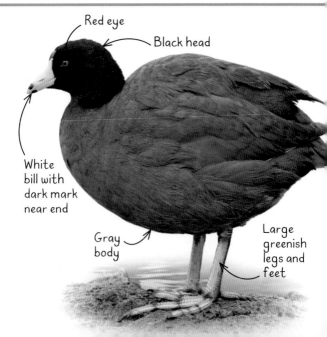

Red eye

Black head

White bill with dark mark near end

Gray body

Large greenish legs and feet

Pied-billed Grebe

This is the most common grebe in North America. It can be found in small ponds and marshes anywhere except in the far north.

Ponds, marshes

Fish, insects

13 in (35 cm)

Seen it!

American Coot

Young Coots have gray bills and paler bellies. In the winter Coots meet up in groups, which may also include ducks.

Ponds, marshes

Plants, snails, insects

15½ in (40 cm)

Ducklike bird
Coots are not ducks, but they can look like ducks swimming on a pond. Look for the small white bill and black head.

Seen it!

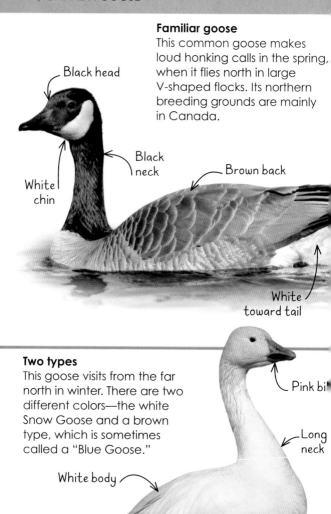

Familiar goose
This common goose makes loud honking calls in the spring, when it flies north in large V-shaped flocks. Its northern breeding grounds are mainly in Canada.

Black head

Black neck

White chin

Brown back

White toward tail

Two types
This goose visits from the far north in winter. There are two different colors—the white Snow Goose and a brown type, which is sometimes called a "Blue Goose."

Pink bi

Long neck

White body

Black wingtips

Pink legs and feet

Canada Goose

These geese are found on lakes and grassy fields all over North America. There are now so many that they are a pest on lawns and golf courses, where they like to feed.

Water, fields

Plants

3 ft (1 m)

Seen it!

Snow Goose

In the fall these birds often have rust-colored heads. This is because the water they feed in during their summer in the north is full of iron.

Marshes, fields

Grass, seeds

30 in (76 cm)

Seen it!

Winter visitor

Look for these birds on lakes and bays in the winter. In the summer, they nest in Arctic tundra in the far north. Young birds travel with their parents and have brown streaks on their heads and necks.

Small yellow spot in front of eye

Long black bill

Long straight neck

All-white body

Tundra Swan

These swans only visit the US in the winter. You might see other types of swans all year round.

Lakes, bays

Plants, seeds

4 ft (1.2 m)

Seen it!

Pale cap

Throat pouch

Large black feet

Good in the air
Pelicans are huge birds and look very clumsy when walking or standing still. But when they fly, pelicans seem to float on the air. They often glide low over the water.

Very large bill

Chunky body

Gray wings

Brown Pelican

Brown Pelicans dive into the water to catch fish, sometimes from over sixty feet in the air. They use their huge bills to scoop up the fish.

Coasts

Fish

4 ft
(1.2 m)

Seen it!

Great dancer
Male and female cranes dance together in the spring. They bow to each other and jump around, making loud bugling calls.

Red cap

Long black bill

Long neck

Gray body

Shaggy tail

Long dark legs

Sandhill Crane

Cranes fly with their long necks held straight and their legs trailing behind. They often call while flying.

Marshes, fields

Plants, snails

3 ft (1 m)

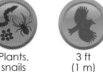
Seen it!

Big bird

This is the largest heron in North America. In the south, some Great Blue Herons are white all over.

Black stripe on head

White face

Long pointy bill

Long gray neck

Gray body

Shaggy feathers on chest

Long pale gray legs

Great Blue Heron

When herons fly they usually hold their long necks tucked in, making an S-shape. They rarely call when flying.

Wetlands

Fish

3 ft (1 m)

Seen it!

Yellow bill

White body

Seen it!

Long neck

Great Egret
Egrets are patient fishermen.
They often stand still for a long
time staring down at the water,
waiting for a fish to swim by.

Black legs
and feet

Green Heron
All Green Herons have the
same chunky shape, but
young ones have brown
backs, streaky bellies, and
white spots on their wings.

Green cap

Green back

Short
brown neck

Yellow legs
and feet

White stripe on
chest and throat

Seen it!

Black-crowned Night-Heron

Night-Herons are nearly twice as big as Green Herons. They feed at night and sit quietly during the day.

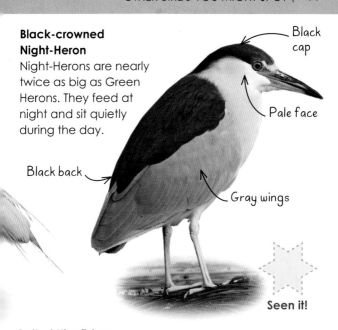

Black cap

Pale face

Black back

Gray wings

Seen it!

Belted Kingfisher

Listen for the loud rattle call of the kingfisher wherever there is water and fish. Females have a rusty band across the belly.

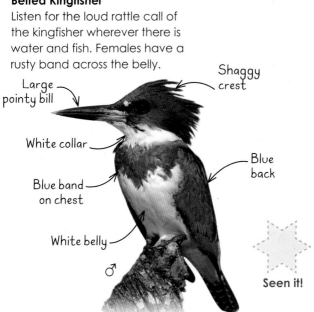

Shaggy crest

Large pointy bill

White collar

Blue back

Blue band on chest

White belly

♂

Seen it!

Smooth divers
Cormorants swim along very low in the water. They dive down head first to catch fish. Young birds have pale necks and chests.

Long neck

Long bill with hooked tip

Black body

Large dark legs and feet

Double-crested Cormorant

You often see a cormorant standing with its wings spread open, as if hanging them out to dry.

Coasts, watersides

Fish

30 in (80 cm)

Seen it!

Sociable bird
Terns are rarely alone.
They almost always
travel and feed in flocks.
They also nest together
in large groups.

Pointy red bill
with black tip

Black cap

Gray back

Gray
belly

Red legs and
feet

Common Tern

These terns dive into the sea for fish.
On lakes, they fly down to the water to
catch insects or tiny fish.

Coasts,
watersides

Fish,
insects

13 in
(33 cm)

Seen it!

Migration

Some birds stay in the same place all year. Others go to different places at different times of the year—this is called migration. Usually, migrating birds move from north to south for the winter, when food becomes harder to find in northern areas.

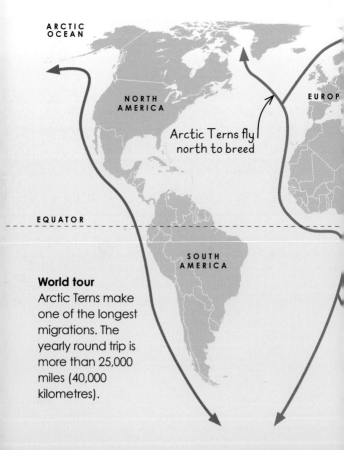

ARCTIC
OCEAN

NORTH
AMERICA

EUROP

Arctic Terns fly
north to breed

EQUATOR

SOUTH
AMERICA

World tour
Arctic Terns make one of the longest migrations. The yearly round trip is more than 25,000 miles (40,000 kilometres).

Arctic to Antarctic

Arctic Terns nest in the far north during the summer when the days are long. In the fall, they migrate south to the Antarctic Ocean where it is summer. They see more daylight than any other bird.

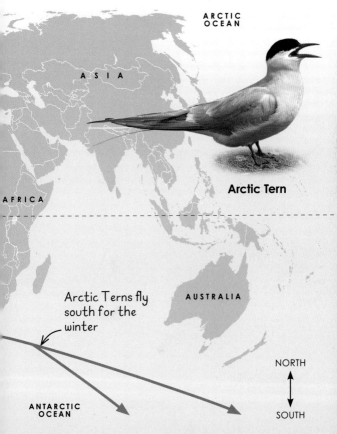

ARCTIC OCEAN

ASIA

AFRICA

Arctic Tern

AUSTRALIA

Arctic Terns fly south for the winter

ANTARCTIC OCEAN

NORTH

SOUTH

Black head

Quiet winter
Listen for these gulls in the spring and summer. In the winter, they are quieter and have black smudges behind their eyes, instead of black heads.

Dark gray back

White neck and belly

Black wing tips

Long dark legs

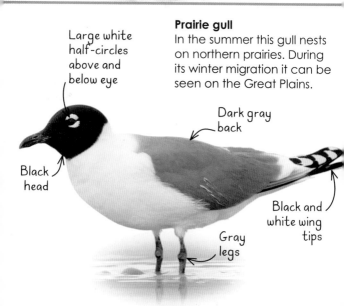

Large white half-circles above and below eye

Prairie gull
In the summer this gull nests on northern prairies. During its winter migration it can be seen on the Great Plains.

Dark gray back

Black head

Black and white wing tips

Gray legs

Laughing Gull

These gulls nest together in large groups in the summer. Their *ha-ha-ha-ha* calls are so loud they can be almost deafening.

Coasts

Insects, small fish

17 in (42 cm)

Seen it!

Franklin's Gull

These gulls often follow plows in fields, looking for worms and insects. They usually look less scruffy than other gulls, because they molt their feathers more often.

Prairies, open fields

Earthworms, insects

13 in (34 cm)

Seen it!

Yellow bill with black ring

White head

Gray back

Black wing tips with white spots

White belly

Yellow or green legs

Confusing birds

Gulls can be confusing because there are several kinds that look like one another. Look at their size and the color o their back, legs, and bills

Large gull

In most places, this is the most common large gull. It takes four years to get its adult colors. Young birds are mostly brown. Adults have streaky heads in winter.

Large yellow bill with red spot

Gray back

White chest and belly

Pink legs

Black wing tips with white spots

Ring-billed Gull

This is the most common medium-sized gull in North America. In the summer it nests inland, near freshwater.

Watersides

Fish, insects, seeds

Seen it!

20 in
(50 cm)

Herring Gull

These birds are one of nature's garbage collectors. They will eat any scraps of food that they can find, and are common at garbage dumps.

Watersides

Fish, shellfish, scraps

Seen it!

24 in
(62 cm)

Greater Yellowlegs
This bird has a loud, whistled *tew*, *tew*, *tew* call. It nests in Alaska and northern Canada.

Brown back with white spots

Long, thin, pointy bill

Pale belly

Long yellow legs

Seen it!

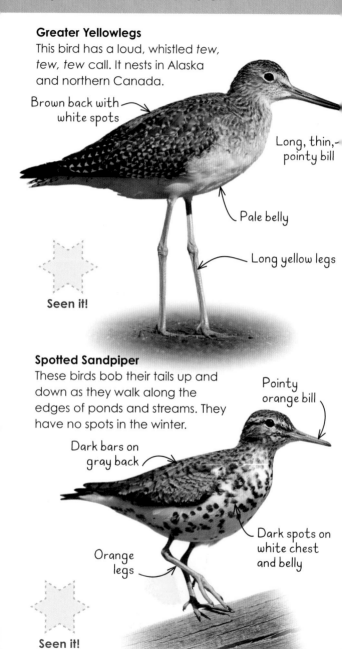

Spotted Sandpiper
These birds bob their tails up and down as they walk along the edges of ponds and streams. They have no spots in the winter.

Pointy orange bill

Dark bars on gray back

Dark spots on white chest and belly

Orange legs

Seen it!

American Woodcock

Look for these shy birds on the edges of wet brushy and wooded areas in the east. They are most active after dark.

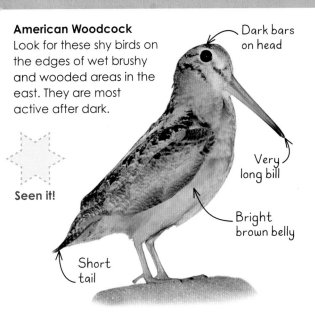

Dark bars on head

Very long bill

Bright brown belly

Short tail

Seen it!

Killdeer

If a predator is close to a Killdeer's nest, the Killdeer pretends to be injured, hoping that the predator will try to catch it instead of finding its eggs or chicks.

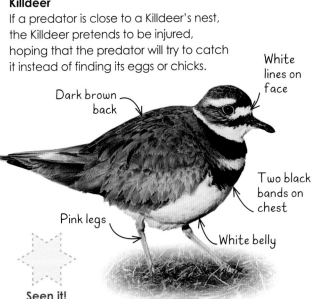

White lines on face

Dark brown back

Two black bands on chest

Pink legs

White belly

Seen it!

Index

Acknowledgments

Dorling Kindersley would like to thank the following: Liz Moore for picture research, Clare McLean for sticker advice, CTS Peter Pawsey, Claire Bowers for DK images, Jacket Design Development Manager Sophia Tampakopoulos, Gill Pitts for editorial help, and Jonny Burrows for design assistance.

The publisher would also like to thank the following for their kind permission to reproduce their photographs: (Key: a-above; b-below/bottom; c-center; f-far; l-left; r-right; t-top)

1 Dorling Kindersley: Garth McElroy (c). 4 Alamy Images: Pick and Mix Images (bl). Getty Images: Tim Graham (cl). 5 Alamy Images: blickwinkel (tr). 7 Dorling Kindersley: Garth McElroy (bl); Bob Steele (crb). 8 Getty Images: John Cornell (ca); George Grall (bc). 9 Corbis: Tero Niemi / Naturbild (tc). 13 Dorling Kindersley: Natural History Museum, London (cl). 16 Dorling Kindersley: Garth McElroy (bc); Alan Murphy (tc). 18 Dorling Kindersley: Brian E. Small (bc). 22 Dorling Kindersley: Brian E. Small (tc, bc). 24 Dorling Kindersley: Bob Steele (cla). 25 Dorling Kindersley: Garth McElroy (ca). 28 Dorling Kindersley: Garth McElroy (tc); Brian E. Small (bc). 30 Dorling Kindersley: Brian E. Small (ca). 31 Dorling Kindersley: Garth McElroy (bc). 33 Dorling Kindersley: Robert Royse (ca). 34 Dorling Kindersley: Garth McElroy (cb). 35 Dorling Kindersley: Brian E. Small (ca). 36 Alamy Images: Marvin Dembinsky Photo Associates (ca). Getty Images: Konrad Wothe (clb). 37 Getty Images: AFP (cb); Burazin (ca). 38 Dorling Kindersley: Brian E. Small (ca). 39 Dorling Kindersley: Brian E. Small (ca). 42 Dorling Kindersley: Brian E. Small (ca). 44 Dorling Kindersley: Garth McElroy (c); Bob Steele (tc). 45 Dorling Kindersley: Garth McElroy (tc); Brian E. Small (c). 46 Dorling Kindersley: Dudley Edmondson (ca); Garth McElroy (ca). 48 Dorling Kindersley: Brian E. Small (ca). 52 Dorling Kindersley: Chris Gomersall (ca); Tom Grey (br). Getty Images: Darrell Gulin (tl); Visuals Unlimited, Inc. / Garth McElroy (c). 56 Dorling Kindersley: Bob Steele (ca). Christopher Taylor: (cb). 58 Dorling Kindersley: Garth McElroy (ca); Brian E. Small (cl). 61 Dorling Kindersley: Brian E. Small (ca). 62 Dorling Kindersley: Brian E. Small (ca, cb). 63 Dorling Kindersley: Brian E. Small (ca, cb). 66 Dorling Kindersley: Bob Steele (ca). 67 Dorling Kindersley: Robert Royse (ca). 68 Alamy Images: Bill Coster (cl). Corbis: Roger Tidman (cb). 69 Getty Images: Guy Edwardes (cb); Donald M. Jones (ca). 70 Dorling Kindersley: Brian E. Small (ca). 72 Dorling Kindersley: E. J. Peiker (ca). 73 Dorling Kindersley: Brian E. Small (ca). 79 Dorling Kindersley: Chris Gomersall Photography (cla). 80 Alamy Images: Richard Mittleman / Gon2Foto (bl). Dorling Kindersley: Garth McElroy (cla). 81 Dorling Kindersley: Brian E. Small (tr). Getty Images: S.J. Krasemann (br). 84 Dorling Kindersley: Markus Varesvuo (ca). 86 Dorling Kindersley: Brian E. Small (ca). 87 Dorling Kindersley: Brian E. Small (cb). 88 Dorling Kindersley: Robert Royse (cb). 90 Dorling Kindersley: Alan Murphy (ca). 95 Dorling Kindersley: Brian E. Small (ca). 96 Dorling Kindersley: Brian E. Small (ca). 98 Dorling Kindersley: Garth McElroy (ca, cb). 99 Dorling Kindersley: Alan Murphy (ca). 103 SuperStock: Science Faction (tl). 104 Dorling Kindersley: Brian E. Small (ca). 108 Dorling Kindersley: Brian E. Small (cb). 109 Dorling Kindersley: Garth McElroy (ca)

Jacket images: Front: Alamy Images: Craig Lovell / Eagle Visions Photography cla; Dorling Kindersley: E. J. Peiker bl, Brian E. Small br; Dreamstime.com: Lokinthru c; Back: Dorling Kindersley: Dudley Edmondson cla, Brian E. Small cra; Spine: Dorling Kindersley: Brian E. Small cb

All other images © Dorling Kindersley
For further information see: **www.dkimages.com**

The author, **Joseph DiCostanzo,** has watched birds for over 40 years. He works at the American Museum of Natural History (AMNH), and has been president of the Linnaean Society of New York, twice. Joe is especially interested in terns, and has studied them with the AMNH's Great Gull Island Project since 1975. He also leads bird walks, and writes books to help other people learn about birds. Joe would like to dedicate this book to Ann.